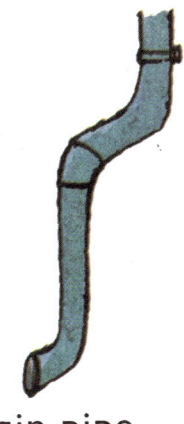

drain pipe

front door

chimney

letter box

window

The house

window box

wall

tree

garage

roof

1

cooker

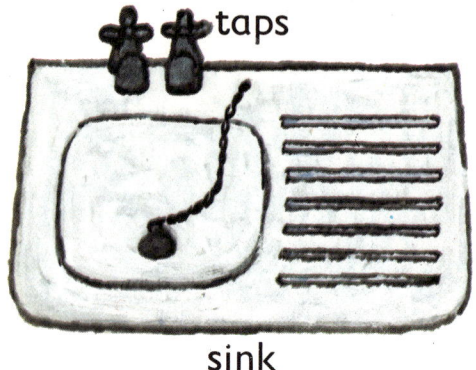

taps

sink

washing machine

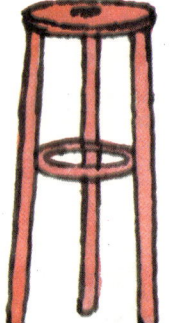

stool

pans

kettle

The kitchen

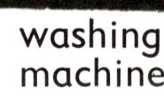

iron

cupboard

fridge

Mother is cooking.

The boy is **sweeping up**.

The girl is ironing.

Father is drying the dishes.

picture

table

chair

cup

saucer

plate

fork

glass

knife

spoon

jug

The dining room

salt and pepper

tray

sideboard

fruit

4

The girl is setting the table.

The boy is eating a banana.

Mother is carrying the tray.

Father is looking at the picture on the wall.

armchair

settee

radio

coffee table

television

The sitting room

cushion

light

carpet

curtains

fire

Father is sitting
in the armchair.

Mother is watching
the television.

The boy is reading
a book.

The girl is closing
the curtains.

radiator

staircase

electricity meter

cloakroom

gas meter

The hall and stairs

telephone

telephone directory

vase of flowers

8

Father is using the telephone.

Mother is going upstairs.

The man is reading the electricity meter.

The girl is hanging her coat in the cloakroom.

bunk beds

wardrobe

cot

teddy

bookcase

toy cupboard

The children's bedroom

pyjamas

slippers

dressing gown

nightdress

10

The baby is sleeping in her cot.

The boy is looking
in the toy cupboard.

Mother is making
the beds.

The girl is reading her book.

bed

wardrobe

dressing table

pillow

shoes

The adults' bedroom

chair

alarm clock

comb

mirror

hairbrush

Father is setting the alarm clock.

Mother is brushing her hair.

The girl is trying on her mother's clothes.

The boy is laughing at the girl.

13

taps

bath

toilet

washbasin

shower

The bathroom

medicine cabinet

soap

toothpaste

towel

toothbrush

shampoo

The girl is
cleaning her teeth.

Father is shaving.

The boy is having a bath.

Mother is
washing her hair.

Things to do

1 Make your own house book about your own home.
Use this book to help you with words.
Draw pictures of things in your own home.
Use photographs and cut pictures from old magazines.
Write as much as you can in your own house book.
Keep a diary for a week about what you do each day.
Make your own book interesting and colourful.
2 Collect pictures of different kinds of homes.
3 Make a list of things in the house made from:
> wood
>
> metal
>
> glass
>
> wool and cotton
4 Act people doing things round the house and guess what they are doing.